FAMOUS IMMIGRANT
ATHLETES

MAKING AMERICA GREAT
IMMIGRANT SUCCESS STORIES

FAMOUS IMMIGRANT
ATHLETES

John A. Torres

Enslow Publishing
101 W. 23rd Street
Suite 240
New York, NY 10011
USA
enslow.com

Published in 2018 by Enslow Publishing, LLC.
101 W. 23rd Street, Suite 240, New York, NY 10011

Library of Congress Cataloging-in-Publication Data

Names: Torres, John Albert, author.
Title: Famous immigrant athletes / by John A. Torres.
Description: New York: Enslow Publishing, [2018] | Series: Making America
great : immigrant success stories | Includes bibliographical references
and index. | Audience: Grades 7–12.
Identifiers: LCCN 2017018587 | ISBN 9780766092433 (library bound) | ISBN 9780766095892
(paperback)
Subjects: LCSH: Athletes—Biography—Juvenile literature. |
Immigrants—Biography—Juvenile literature.
Classification: LCC GV697.A1 T675 2018 | DDC 796.092/2 [B]—dc23
LC record available at https://lccn.loc.gov/2017018587

Printed in the United States of America

Photo credits: Cover, p. 3 Jason O. Watson/Getty Images; p. 7 Underwood Archives/Archive Photos/
Getty Images; pp. 10, 16–17 © AP Images; p. 12 Junior D. Kannah/AFP/Getty Images; p. 20 Rob Tringali/
Getty Images; pp. 22–23 photopixel/Shutterstock.com; pp. 26–27 Philip Scalia/Alamy Stock Photo; p. 31
Staff/AFP/Getty Images; pp. 32–33 AFP/Getty Images; pp. 36–37 Gerry Cranham/Science Source/
Getty Images; pp. 38–39 John Moore/Getty Images; p. 42 Dirck Halstead/The LIFE Images Collection/
Getty Images; p. 43 Imagno/Hulton Archive/Getty Images; pp. 46–47 Julia Davila-Lampe/Moment/
Getty Images; p. 49 Hulton Archive/Archive Photos/Getty Images; p. 51 World History Archive/
Alamy Stock Photo; p. 53 Mandel Ngan/AFP/Getty Images; p. 55 Darlene Hammond/Archive Photos/
Getty Images; p. 57 William Purnell/Icon Sportswire/Getty Images; p. 59 Brendan van Son/Moment/
Getty Images; p. 61 Francois Rojon/AFP/Getty Images; p. 63 Centre Daily Times/Tribune News
Service/Getty Images; p. 67 Bongarts/Getty Images; pp. 68–69 Igor Kostin/Sygma/Getty Images;
pp. 72–73 EMPICS Sport/PA Images/Getty Images; pp. 74–75 Aleksandrs Tihonovs/Alamy Stock Photo;
p. 79 Sporting News/Getty Images; pp. 82–83 Georgetown University/Collegiate Images/Getty Images;
p. 87 Jim McIsaac/Getty Images; pp. 88–89 Art Rickerby/The LIFE Picture Collection/Getty Images;
pp. 90–91 John Seaton Callahan/Moment/Getty Images; pp. 94–95 Kyodo News/Getty Images; cover
and interior pages Saicle/Shutterstock.com (flag).

Contents

Introduction

Since its founding in 1776, the United States has been a nation of immigrants. In fact, the diversity in the United States makes it one of the most unique countries in the world. America is a place where newcomers can come with nothing and make their dreams come true. Some of these new arrivals have run from countries where they've faced war, hunger, or mistreatment because of their race or religion. In the United States, they restart their lives and give back to their new country.

Immigrants have touched every area of life in America, including the professional sports world. They have led basketball teams to the NBA championships and baseball teams to the World Series. They've even won Olympic gold medals for their new country.

Famous immigrant athletes include basketball superstar Yao Ming and bodybuilder Arnold Schwarzenegger. Both achieved greatness as athletes in their home countries, allowing them to move to the United States and become even more successful in sports. Schwarzenegger, for example, became a movie star and, later, the governor of California.

Other immigrant athletes, such as baseball sluggers Jose Canseco and Albert Pujols, wowed fans with their home runs. Immigrants have made a huge impact on baseball, so much so that more than three hundred players who took part in the 2016 Major League Baseball season were born outside the United States. Altogether, they represented more than twenty-two different countries.[1]

For years, Major League Baseball has attracted immigrants from all over the world. In 1999, Tommy Lasorda, then baseball manager of the Los Angeles Dodgers, told the Associated Press, "For

Often escaping war, poverty, and disease, immigrants from around the world packed their meager belongings and set out for the land of opportunity—the United States.

starting pitchers we have two Dominicans, one Italian, one Mexican and one Japanese. In the bullpen we have a Venezuelan, a Mexican, a guy from the United States and a guy from St. Louis."[2]

Individual sports, such as tennis, have also attracted immigrants. In 2017, *USA Today* published a feature article about three young immigrant tennis players, all of whom expressed excitement about the opportunity to represent "the red, white, and blue." Tennis officials welcomed the three youngsters because of their much-needed talent.

Michael Mmoh, was born in Saudi Arabia to a Nigerian father and an Irish and Australian mother. Now he lives and trains in the United States. "I've been playing for the States my entire career," Mmoh told *USA Today*. "The [U.S. Tennis Association] supports me a lot and I like all the coaches, and I like the entire organization and feel they support me really well. There's no other country I'd play for."[3]

Mmoh is not alone. In this book, you'll read about some of the most famous immigrants ever to succeed in professional sports in the United States. Learn how their contributions as athletes have made history.

CHAPTER 1

DIKEMBE MUTOMBO

A gentle giant, Dikembe Mutombo remained popular well past his basketball days because of his big grin and distinct finger wag. Not only have many people tried to copy his finger wag over the years, but the gesture has also been featured in television shows, movies, and commercials.

During his career as an intimidating NBA center, Mutombo made his mark as an eight-time all-star and four-time defensive player of the year. After he retired in 2009, Mutombo was inducted into the Naismith Memorial Basketball Hall of Fame.

In retirement, Mutombo has completed charity work that has made a lasting impact on the world. But when he was born on January 25, 1966, in Kinshasa, Zaire (now the Democratic Republic of the Congo), he faced challenges. Likely no one from his hometown imagined that the little boy would leave such a mark on the world, as the city had high crime and poverty rates.[1]

GROWING UP

Given the birth name of Dikembe Mutombo Mpolondo Mukamba Jean Jacque Wamutombo, the future basketball star belonged to an upper-class family. He grew up in a six-bedroom house with four

Zaire native Dikembe Mutombo used a physical style of play to make his mark in the NBA. Here, he is driving to the hoop during a 1997 game against the Portland Trail Blazers.

brothers and two sisters. His father, educated in France, oversaw the city's high schools. And both education and discipline were valued in the Mutombo household.[2] Like his brothers and sisters, Dikembe learned to speak many languages as a boy, including French, Spanish, English, Portuguese, and numerous African dialects.

He also excelled at soccer, a popular sport in many countries, including a variety of African nations. Although Dikembe was very tall, he thrived as a soccer goalkeeper and in martial arts. By the time he enrolled in high school, Dikembe grew to be 7 feet (213 centimeters) tall and was a great goalkeeper for the school team.

THE DEMOCRATIC REPUBLIC OF THE CONGO

The Democratic Republic of the Congo is a central African country known by many different names over the years. Before 1908, it was known as the Congo Free State. From 1908 until 1960, it was known as the Belgian Congo. Since then, it has been known as the Republic of Congo, Congo-Leopoldville, and Zaire.

The country was a Belgian colony for many years, and Europeans stripped the country of many of its natural resources, such as gold, diamonds, and oil. The Democratic Republic of the Congo, which shares borders with Uganda, Rwanda, Sudan, Burundi, Tanzania, Zambia, the Central African Republic, and Angola, won its independence from Belgium in 1960.

Unfortunately, political corruption and instability have caused the fourth most populous African nation to suffer through several civil wars, crime, and poverty. Civil wars in the 1990s

(continued on the next page)

(continued from the previous page)

A boy fishes while on the Kwenge River in the Democratic Republic of Congo. Due to political instability and poverty, many in the country have to rely on the land and the country's resources for their food.

caused many foreign businesspeople and companies to leave the country. While the country still has a rich supply of natural resources, it has also seen famine and disease. Children under age five often fall ill, making up half of the Congo's deaths.

Yet, Dikembe Mutombo survived his early childhood to become an internationally famous basketball star. He's not the only one. Professional basketball players like Serge Ibaka, Bismack Biyombo, Christian Eyenga, and Emmanuel Mudiay are from the Congo. In addition to basketball and soccer, rugby is a popular sport in the country.

Dikembe hesitated to play basketball. When he finally tried the sport, he was awkward, not very good, and even cracked his chin during a fall.[3] He wanted to quit the sport, but his father told him to keep trying.

Soon, he got the hang of the game and found that his great height was a big advantage. It allowed him to grab rebounds, protect his own net, and block shot after shot attempt by the opposing team. He began playing for the country's national team but dreamed of attending college in the United States.

As a member of the national team, where he played alongside one of his brothers, Mutombo traveled a lot, which sparked his interest in different countries. During a visit to the US embassy, Mutombo caught the eye of an embassy employee who was friends with college basketball coach John Thompson. The famous coach had turned the Georgetown Hoyas into one of the best teams in the Big East Conference.[4] The chance encounter with Thompson's friend would change Mutombo's life.

US BOUND

At age twenty-one, Mutombo moved to the United States to become a student at Georgetown University. He arrived with two pairs of pants, three shirts, and a dream that he would become a doctor and go back to the Congo to help his people. He spent his first year at the university improving his English, taking classes, and playing basketball for fun.

But just about everyone urged the gentle giant to speak with Thompson about playing on the basketball team. When they finally met, Thompson convinced Mutombo that he could make a greater impact on the world by playing basketball than he could by being a doctor.[5]

He joined the team, but the learning curve was pretty tough. On the court he often faced off against teammate and future friend Alonzo Mourning, already one of the best college centers in the country. Mutombo grew frustrated when Mourning played better than he did. He also struggled to get used to life at Georgetown, especially with a tough coach like Thompson who cared as much about sports as he did about education. For instance, after Mutombo missed a day of classes to take care of a terrible toothache, Thompson threatened to remove him from the team if he skipped class again without telling him first.

"Coach really didn't take no prisoner. It was his way, or no other way. You were here to play basketball but you also had to go to class. If you didn't, you were in trouble," Mutombo said.[6]

Soon enough, Mutombo found his groove. Along with Mourning, the duo dominated games defensively. Mutombo once even blocked twelve shots in a single game. By the time he was a sophomore, he believed he might be able to play in the NBA. His time at Georgetown prepared him for a career in professional basketball as well as for careers away from the game. He spent one summer as an intern for Congress and another as an intern for the World Bank.

But basketball was his fate. In 1991, the Denver Nuggets had the fourth overall pick in the NBA draft and chose Mutombo. This was an amazing turn of events for a man who hadn't started playing basketball until high school. Known as the worst defensive team in the league, however, the Nuggets needed a shot-blocking specialist like Mutombo on their team.

He made an immediate impact in the league and won a spot on the all-star team. Then, he started making his famous finger-wagging gesture whenever he would block a shot, sometimes adding the words "no, no, no." The finger wag became so popular that Mutombo appeared in television ads doing it.

That was hardly Mutombo's only accomplishment. During his second season in the league, Mutombo helped lead the normally terrible Denver Nuggets to a spot in the play-offs. During the next few seasons, Mutombo continued to improve, but his team never won a championship. In fact, the Nuggets never made it past the second round of the play-offs.

Still, the big man from Africa loved Denver and wanted to stay. When his contract expired, he asked the team to give him some stability by offering him a ten-year contract. But the team refused, so Mutombo signed a deal with the Atlanta Hawks. Bernie Bickerstaff, then the general manager of the Nuggets, later said that the biggest regret of his entire career was letting Mutombo leave Denver.[7]

In 1997, Mutombo lost his mother. She died of a stroke in Congo. Her death gave him the desire to give back, which he would later do in his native country.

THE MOUNTAIN

Nicknamed "Mt. Mutombo" because of his size, Mutombo helped lead the Hawks to back-to-back fifty-win seasons and good play-off runs. He would later be traded to the Philadelphia 76ers, where he led the team to the NBA Finals. Sadly for Mutombo, his team lost to the Los Angeles Lakers. Altogether, Mutombo played for eighteen seasons in the NBA, enjoying stints with the New York Knicks, New Jersey Nets, Chicago Bulls, and Houston Rockets before retiring in 2009.

Mutombo realized fairly early in his career that his college basketball coach John Thompson was right. Mutombo could affect more people's lives as a pro basketball player than he could as a doctor. In 1997, he started the Dikembe Mutombo Foundation to improve living conditions for the poor in the Democratic Republic of the Congo.

But the athlete has also taken part in charitable work outside of Congo. A humanitarian in the truest sense, Mutombo has participated in Basketball Without Borders and served as a spokesman for CARE, an international relief agency that focuses on children's health and safety throughout the world.

THE SPECIAL OLYMPICS

The international competitive games for athletes suffering from intellectual disabilities, known as the Special Olympics, started in 1968. Eunice Kennedy Shriver founded the organization. It started as a camp at her home because she feared that children with these disabilities had no one to play with and nowhere to play.

During the same period that Shriver founded the Special Olympics, several important doctors and researchers performed studies that found that people with intellectual disabilities benefit from exercise and physical activity. So, the first Special Olympics took place in 1968 at Soldier Field in Chicago. American and Canadian athletes with disabilities competed in swimming, track and field, and floor hockey matches.

To say the games have grown a great deal since then would be an understatement. The games took place in the United States until 2003, when the Special Olympics grew into an international event. That year, Dublin, Ireland, hosted the games, which featured 7,000 athletes from 150 different countries. The games have grown even more since then.

Nearly 5.5 million athletes in 170 countries participate in some sort of Special Olympics program or training. Any athlete age eight and up with an intellectual disability, such as autism or Down syndrome, may take part in the games for free. Some of the sports offered include kayaking, track and field, sailing, tennis, basketball, softball, volleyball, and golf.

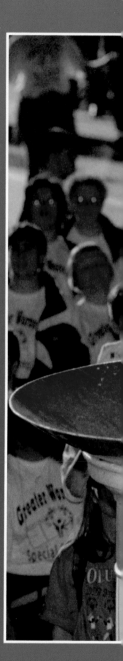

The torch representing the fire of competition, the Olympic flame, is lit to signify the start of the 1997 Special Olympics held in Boston, Massachusetts.

Mutombo has also been a longtime supporter of the Special Olympics, serving as a goodwill ambassador and on the International Board of Directors, and he has been a leader in the Unified Sports movement. In Unified Sports, athletes with intellectual disabilities are paired up with athletes without disabilities during competition. Mutombo has played in at least two Unified Sports Soccer tournaments, using the skills he learned as a child on the soccer field. The athlete stands out because he doesn't simply lend his name or money to a cause but takes part as well.

In 2007, President George W. Bush invited Mutombo to attend his 2007 State of the Union Address. Mutombo considers the honor one of the greatest of his life. Describing Mutombo, Bush said:

"Dikembe became a star in the NBA, and a citizen of the United States. But he never forgot the land of his birth, or the duty to share his blessings with others. He built a brand new hospital in his old hometown. A friend has said of this good-hearted man, 'Mutombo believes that God has given him this opportunity to do great things.' And we are proud to call this son of the Congo a citizen of the United States of America."[8]

As he listened to Bush's speech, Mutombo almost started to cry. He later said he was overjoyed that the president would honor him with such praise.[9] But Mutombo deserved it. He managed to raise and contribute enough money to build the first new hospital in Kinshasa, Congo, in more than forty years. The Biamba Marie Mutombo Hospital and Research Center bears his mother's name.

CHAPTER 2

ALBERT PUJOLS

Albert Pujols's childhood sounds like a Hollywood movie. Too poor to purchase the equipment needed to play baseball, he used limes in place of balls and a milk carton for his glove. Despite these hardships, Pujols's natural talent shined through, and he turned out to be one of the greatest home-run hitters of all time.

Jose Alberto Pujols Alcantara was born on January 16, 1980, in the capital city of Santo Domingo in the Dominican Republic. The DR, as it is often called, sits on the Caribbean island of Hispaniola. Haiti, the poorest country in the Western Hemisphere, also calls the island home.

BROKEN HOME

In addition to growing up in a very poor section of Santo Domingo, Albert had other challenges to overcome early in life. His parents divorced when he was very young, and he had very little contact with his mother. His father was a minor league pitcher in the Dominican Republic and was often away from home. So Albert's grandmother raised him in an already crowded house filled with cousins, uncles, and aunts.

The family depended on government assistance to afford food and other basic needs,[1] but love and affection filled the household. Albert enjoyed his

Baseball slugger Albert Pujols has been one of the game's most feared and respected home-run hitters for nearly two decades. He has played for both the Cardinals and the Angels.

childhood, which he spent much of playing outside because so many people lived in his home. Albert and his friends often played baseball in empty fields, as Dominicans have long loved the sport.

Of course, they often had to use fruit for baseballs because they could not afford to buy real ones. They would also make baseball mitts out of cartons.[2] Baseball bats were the easiest piece of equipment to find. Any tree branch would do.

THE DOMINICAN REPUBLIC AND BASEBALL

For centuries, Native peoples known as the Taíno lived on the island of Hispaniola, home to both the Dominican Republic and Haiti. When Spanish explorer Christopher Columbus reached Hispaniola in 1492 as many as three million Taínos lived there. They welcomed Columbus and his crew, but many died after contracting diseases, such as smallpox and measles, from the newcomers. Just fifty years after Columbus's arrival, very few Taínos remained.

The decimation of the Taíno is not the only difficulty the Dominican Republic has experienced. The nation has gone to war with Haiti and lost power to the English and the Spaniards at times. American soldiers twice occupied the country.

So, just how did baseball become the most popular sport in the republic? The English introduced Dominicans to the game of cricket, which shares some similarities with baseball. But it wasn't until the arrival of baseball-loving Cubans (fleeing war at home in

(continued on the next page)

(continued from the previous page)

the 1870s) that Dominicans widely became fond of the sport.

By 1890, the first professional Dominican baseball league started and gained a large following throughout the country. In 1956, Osvaldo Virgil became the first Dominican to play Major League Baseball. In the years that followed, the Dominican Republic has earned a reputation for producing great baseball players. Since Virgil's debut, more than four hundred Dominicans have played Major League Baseball, including Pujols, Sammy Sosa, Pedro Martinez, and Hall of Fame pitcher Juan Marichal.

But the athletes who choose to play in the Dominican Republic have left their mark on the game as well. Over the years, the Dominican national team has won numerous medals during global competition, including going undefeated during the 2013 World Baseball Classic.

Today, the Dominican baseball season takes place during the winter, which allows Dominican players to participate in both the national team and the major leagues, if they please. Also, many American players, especially younger athletes looking for more experience, play in the Dominican league during Major League Baseball's off season.

The Dominican Republic, home to scenic mountain views and white-sand beaches, has produced a great number of Major League Baseball stars over the years.

Before long, Albert became obsessed with baseball. When he wasn't outside playing the sport himself, he liked watching his father play. He also loved to watch baseball on television. The Atlanta Braves were the only Major League Baseball team with games broadcast on Dominican television, so Pujols became a fan.

On the empty fields of Santo Domingo, Albert soon discovered that he could hit baseballs—and he could hit them very far.

A BIG MOVE

By age thirteen, Albert was playing baseball with real equipment against much older athletes, some of whom could pitch the ball at 90 miles (145 kilometers) per hour. He said it forced him to become older mentally.[3] Three years later, however, his family moved to New York City. Since the city has a large Dominican population, they thought they could find a better life. Plus, many people in the Big Apple speak Spanish, so they figured they could easily fit in there.

But within a few months of the family's move, Albert witnessed a shooting at a grocery store. The crime shocked his family, who decided to move to a safer place.[4] They ended up in Missouri, a state with few Dominicans and a small percentage of Spanish speakers. Pujols struggled when his high school gave him an English tutor who spoke no Spanish, since he spoke no English. At that moment, he wished he lived anywhere but Missouri.[5]

Communicating with people in his new state proved difficult, but Albert quickly made a name for himself on the baseball field. During his senior year, he crushed eight home runs in only thirty-three at-bats. He came to the plate fifty-five more times, but the coaches of rival pitchers ordered them to walk him on purpose. Many people believed Albert was older than eighteen and should not have been playing against high school kids. This rumor bothered him for years.

Pujols went on to play baseball at Maple Woods Community College in Kansas City, Missouri. During his second season there, he batted an incredible .461 with twenty-two home runs. Hopes were high that he'd be drafted in the first few rounds of the 1999 Major League Baseball amateur draft, but he was not chosen until the thirteenth round. That's because some teams believed the rumor that he was older than his age. Fernando Arango, a scout for the Tampa Bay Rays, pleaded with his team to draft Pujols. He told them Pujols would be an outstanding player.

But they ignored his pleas, leading Arango to quit working for them.[6]

DRAFTED

Ultimately, the St. Louis Cardinals drafted Pujols and gave him a bonus of $60,000. After his first season in the minor leagues, Pujols won the league's Most Valuable Player award. Before long, Pujols graduated from the minor leagues to the major leagues.

He experienced changes in his personal life as well. In 2000, Pujols married his wife, Deidre. Together, they have five children and live in St. Louis between baseball seasons.

Pujols struck so much fear into the competition as a hitter during his minor league career that by 2001, the Cardinals wondered how he could benefit their team. Even though the team had no real openings, the Cardinals made room for him in the lineup by moving him around to different positions. One day he would play first base; the next day he would play third base. He also filled in as a right or left fielder.

He smashed more than twenty home runs by July and became the first Cardinals rookie to make the All-Star team. He finished the season with thirty-seven homers and 130 runs. He not only won the Rookie of the Year award but also finished fourth in the voting for the National League's Most Valuable Player. When Pujols retires, he will likely win a spot in the Baseball Hall of Fame.

THE BASEBALL HALL OF FAME

The National Baseball Hall of Fame in Cooperstown, New York, preserves baseball history and the achievements of its greatest players. The Hall of Fame's motto is "Preserving History, Honoring Excellence, Connecting Generations." It opened in 1939, in part, to draw more people to local hotels. But it soon became the most serious and respected of the halls of fame.

Players can make it into the hall in one of two ways: the Baseball Writers Association of America can vote them in within five years of their retirement or the Veteran's Committee may vote them in if the writers fail to do so within a certain time frame. The hall's first inductees included all-time greats Babe Ruth, Ty Cobb, Honus Wagner, Walter Johnson, and Christy Mathewson. Currently, a few players are inducted into the hall of fame annually. The museum and hall attract about three hundred thousand visitors each year.

At least two players who would have normally been shoo-ins for induction into the Hall of Fame were banned because of their conduct off field. "Shoeless" Joe Jackson faced claims that he took money to lose the 1919

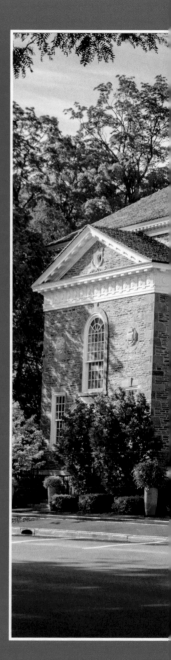

(continued on page 28)

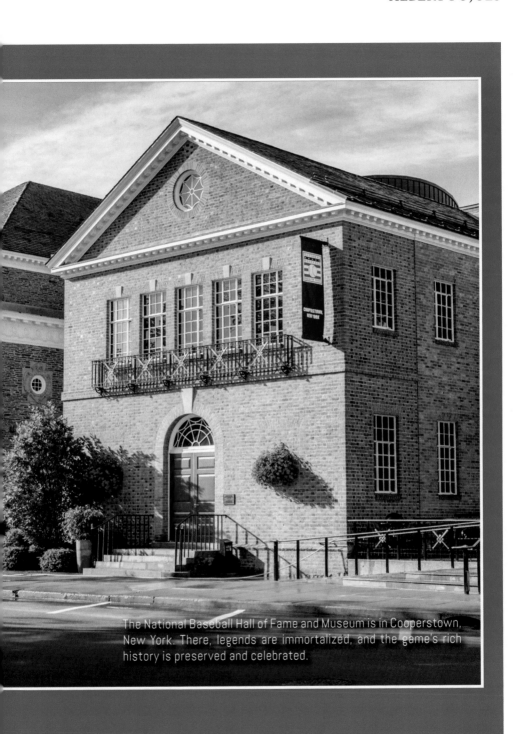

The National Baseball Hall of Fame and Museum is in Cooperstown, New York. There, legends are immortalized, and the game's rich history is preserved and celebrated.

(continued from page 26)

World Series on purpose. Pete Rose, an all-time hits leader in baseball, admitted to betting on baseball games while managing the Cincinnati Reds following his retirement as a player.

In recent years, the baseball writers have refused to vote in great players like Roger Clemens, Mark McGwire, and Sammy Sosa, among others, because of their suspected use of steroids.

THE MACHINE

Pujols established himself as one of baseball's leading home-run hitters, blasting at least thirty dingers every year for the next eleven seasons and at least ninety-nine runs in each year of that same span. Pujols stands out from other power hitters because he also hit for a very high average and became one of the game's best-fielding first basemen. That is a very rare combination. He batted .359 in 2003 to lead the league and .357 in 2008. He won the Gold Glove award for being the greatest fielder at his position in 2006 and 2010. For these incredible efforts, Pujols received the National League's Most Valuable Player award in 2005, 2008, and 2009.

During a time when baseball sluggers faced criticism for using steroids and other performance-enhancing drugs, Pujols always maintained a clean image and offered to be tested for those banned substances at any time. So, how does he do it? How does he maintain his power, his fielding, and his high batting average?

He has worked his entire career to keep his swing the same every time he's up to bat. His technique has earned him the nickname "the Machine." Described as "savage and smooth," Pujols's swing comes from his near-perfect form.[7] That perfect swing allowed Pujols to lead the Cardinals to two World Series victories in 2006 and 2011.

Pujols relies on his Christian faith to help him weather challenges in both his career and his personal life. His religious beliefs also motivate him to give back to the public. In particular, he does a lot of work for children born with Down syndrome. His daughter Isabella has the condition.

Through the Pujols Family Foundation, which he started with his wife, the athlete devotes time and money to several different causes, including people with disabilities and serious medical conditions. The organization also helps the poor in his native country, the Dominican Republic. Pujols has worked to bring doctors and dentists to the poorer areas of the island for medical clinics. He's hosted and organized charity golf tournaments as well.

In 2007, Pujols became a US citizen. He earned a perfect score on the citizenship exam.

Although it broke the hearts of St. Louis Cardinals fans, Pujols decided to leave the team after eleven seasons in St. Louis. In 2012, he signed a ten-year contract with the Los Angeles Angels of Anaheim, an American League team. As an Angel, he continues to hit home runs and terrify pitchers with his perfect swing. In 2016, Pujols participated in the All-Star Game, his first as an American League player and his twelfth overall. It likely won't be his last.

CHAPTER 3

MARTINA NAVRATILOVA

Like many immigrant athletes who have achieved great success, Martina Navratilova had a very tough childhood. The legendary tennis star was born Martina Subertova on October 18, 1956, in Czechoslovakia. Both of her parents were athletic. Her mother excelled at gymnastics, tennis, and skiing, and her father worked as a ski instructor.

Her parents divorced when she was just three years old. Her father, who suffered from depression, committed suicide five years later. Her mother remarried, and Martina took her stepfather's last name. He happened to be a tennis coach, which would set the stage for the rest of her life.

LIVING IN SADNESS

Martina Navratilova grew up under strict communist rule because the Soviet Union—where people had few individual rights—basically controlled Czechoslovakia. As a result, Martina said her mother lived in sadness for much of her life.[1] Czechoslovakians could not travel or leave the country when they wanted. They could not speak out against the government or own land. The government divided the property of Martina's mother, allowing many other families to share the grounds.

Fortunately, Martina found tennis early, which

Czech native and tennis legend Martina Navratilova celebrates in 1982 after winning her third singles championship at Wimbledon—one of the most prestigious tournaments in the world.

kept up her spirits. At age four, she spent her free time hitting tennis balls against a cement wall. Three years later, she visited the tennis court regularly. Often, Martina only felt happy when she stepped onto the tennis court and felt the red clay crunch beneath her feet and the thrill of smacking a tennis ball over the net.[2]

THE SOVIET UNION

The Soviet Union, or USSR, was made up of communist nations that united together and formed a superpower under Russian rule. The union formed in 1922 as the Communist Party rose to power in Russia. The party billed itself as a champion of the workers and the peasants but took matters to extremes.

Dictator Joseph Stalin enforced strict rules for people living in the Soviet Union. They could not own land and had to share their wealth with the government, which then dispersed their resources. Stalin ruled with fear and terror. He jailed or killed his opponents and anyone who spoke out against his policies or the government. Many times these critics, known as dissidents, ended up in gulags, or work camps, in Siberia—the coldest and harshest area of Russia.

After World War II, the Soviets seized much of Eastern Europe, including half of Germany. A wall divided the middle of Berlin, keeping the West Germans and East Germans separated. The Soviets not only ruled East Germany but also Czechoslovakia—the birthplace of Martina Navratilova.

With so many countries under its control, the Soviet Union became a feared and powerful government. This caused a lot of tension between the Soviets and Western countries, especially the United States. This conflict led to the cold war, in which the two countries had war-like relations with one another for many years. Over time, residents of the Soviet Union tried defecting, or escaping, to Western countries to live free of harsh government rule.

Ruthless dictator Joseph Stalin ruled the Soviet Union with an iron fist. He instituted a reign of terror and fear among his own people and caused a deadly famine by confiscating farmland and building factories instead.

REFUGE AND SALVATION

Tennis became Martina's main hope in life. And with the help of her stepfather, she learned to play the sport very well. By the time she was a teenager, Martina won tournaments against other teens on a regular basis. She felt as if tennis could be her future.

Living under communist rule, she would never enjoy a rewarding tennis career unless she took action. By the age of fifteen, she became Czechoslovakia's national tennis champion. Under the watchful eye of the Soviets, she played in tournaments around the world. These competitions included the French Open and the Australian Open, where she reached the finals in 1975.

Later that year, during the summer, she made a decision that would change her life forever. After arriving in the United States to participate in the US Open, her love for the country deepened. "When I reached America there was so much space and color," she told a newspaper in 2003. "The possibilities seemed endless. At least that's how I felt at 18."[3]

So, Navratilova decided to seek political asylum. In other words, she escaped from her chaperons and abandoned her country to live in the United States. The FBI guarded her, and US government officials questioned her. Navratilova said she'd grown tired of having her communist government give her orders and take her earnings away. The Czech government, for example, took away all of the prize money she earned from her tennis victories. She'd also clashed with the government when she stayed a few extra days at a tournament, disobeying orders to return home.[4]

The United States understood the difficulties she'd experienced and granted her asylum, or protection in the country. Navratilova was now an American, but she almost became a British citizen. In 1974, the Soviets allowed Navratilova's family to visit her in England while she participated in the Wimbledon tennis tournament. They planned to defect and seek asylum there as a family. But when the moment came, they all lost their nerve.[5]

The next year would not be an easy one for the eighteen-year-old. Czechoslovakia publicly denounced Navratilova, and she feared that she'd never see her mother, stepfather, and siblings again. She was a teenager in a strange country with no family.

These circumstances likely contributed to her having a terrible year on the court. She was cut in the first round of the US Open and did not win any major tournaments. She felt lost but never wondered if she'd made the right decision. The next year, she worked hard and built a career in tennis that would have many calling her the best female player to swing a racquet.

BREAKOUT

In 1978, Navratilova became a breakout star in tennis after beating Chris Evert in the finals at Wimbledon. The win earned her the honor of being the top-ranked female tennis player in the world. The following year, she beat Evert in the Wimbledon finals again.

In 1981, Navratilova won the Australian Open, her third major title. The next year, she won both the French Open and Wimbledon titles. Most tennis players never achieve such success, but Navratilova wasn't satisfied. She began training with Nancy Lieberman, one of the greatest female basketball players of all time. Navratilova wanted to gain more stamina and strength. Her efforts paid off.

In 1983, she posted an incredible mark of 86–1 and took home three more majors: the US Open, the Australian Open, and Wimbledon. From 1982 to 1986, Navratilova lost only six matches and won seventy-four in a row, setting a record. She even defeated

Chris Evert and Martina Navratilova entertained tennis fans for years with their intense rivalry on the court. Many regarded Evert as the second-best player of her generation, behind Navratilova.

Chris Evert, the world's second best player and her only real rival, thirteen times straight during that time frame.

ROLE MODEL

Navratilova became a US citizen in 1981, the same year that she announced that she was bisexual. She would later reveal that she was a lesbian, making her one of the first professional athletes to come out as gay. The LGBTQ community largely views her as a role model. The *Guardian* newspaper of London called Navratilova both the most famous out lesbian and the greatest women's tennis player of all time.[6]

But being gay wasn't always easy for Navratilova. Many hecklers taunted her, and she experienced antigay bigotry firsthand.

She continued playing tennis and winning matches professionally until 2006, when she retired. A dozen years earlier she'd stopped participating full-time on the professional singles tour. And in 2000 she was voted into the International Tennis Hall of Fame.

Her career record is so impressive that it actually looks like a misprint: 1,442–219. That means she won nearly 90 percent of all of her matches. Navratilova also won eighteen major titles, including nine championships at Wimbledon. She was also a great doubles player, winning 177 doubles titles.

Already considered a heroine for escaping communist rule, coming out as a lesbian, and her incredible tennis career, Navratilova won more fans when she made her battle against breast cancer public. During a routine medical checkup in 2010, Navratilova learned she had a tumor in her breast. She had it removed surgically and continued treatments. She announced her diagnosis even though she knew it would result in dozens of interview requests and media appearances. She felt it was too important of an issue to ignore.

HOW TO BECOME AN AMERICAN CITIZEN

People are typically citizens of their countries of birth, but those seeking to be citizens of other countries have options. To become a US citizen, applicants need to move to the country and take up legal residence. After living in America legally for five years, residents can then apply for citizenship. Applicants must be at least eighteen years old and able to pass an English test. They also have to be known as a person of "good moral character"; this means they have not broken any serious laws or engaged in wrongdoing.

Then applicants must take a class on American history and civics. They also complete an in-depth interview with immigration officials before taking and passing an exam on history and civics. The last step involves taking an oath swearing allegiance to the United States.

But other paths also lead to citizenship. Someone can live in the US legally and then marry an American. Keep in mind that immigration officials often do inspections and make surprise visits to ensure that the relationship is real.

Another way to become a citizen is to serve in the US military for at least one year, be in good standing with the armed forces, or be discharged honorably. The applicant must then live in the United States before going through the interviews, classes, and exam. In honor of this service, the government often speeds up the citizenship process for immigrants in the military.

A group of immigrants take the oath to become US citizens during a 2016 ceremony on New York's Ellis Island, once the main portal for immigrants entering the country.

"I want to save lives by telling women to go for the test, and be vigilant, but there is a cost to me, for sure. Last week I did 20 interviews straight and the following evening, when I played tennis, I was exhausted, but it was emotional, not physical, exhaustion," she told a newspaper.[7]

The tennis legend successfully defeated cancer and continues to be an advocate for women's health issues. Since retiring from professional tennis, Navratilova has remained extremely active. She spends much of her time working with charities to help children, protect animals, and more. She is also the health and fitness ambassador for AARP, an organization that benefits senior citizens.

Of course, she remains a role model in the gay community and is a gay rights activist. When asked about her activism, Navratilova points to her childhood and how she grew up in a country with very strict rules. She said she hates discrimination and stupid rules and will always fight against them.[8]

This amazing immigrant is one of the most influential athletes in American history.

CHAPTER 4

ARNOLD
SCHWARZENEGGER

Today, most Americans know Arnold Schwarzenegger as a famous Hollywood action star and former governor of California. But this Austrian-born immigrant made a name for himself as one of the top athletes in his field before he donned a leather jacket and sunglasses as the Terminator and warned, "I'll be back."

Schwarzenegger's career didn't start in Hollywood. Once upon a time, he won the title Mr. Universe. The accomplishment was huge given his early years in a struggling family.

Arnold Alois Schwarzenegger was born July 30, 1947, to parents Gustav and Aurelia in the village of Thal, in the Austrian state of Styria. Thal is a small village with breathtaking views of mountains, lakes, and streams. Despite the beauty of his birthplace, Schwarzenegger faced difficulties.

SCAVENGING FOR FOOD

Gustav Schwarzenegger, briefly a member of the Nazi Party during World War II, was Thal's chief of police. Austria joined forces with Nazi Germany, which was eventually defeated by the United States and its allies.

Austria lacked jobs, food, and other resources. Sometimes riots broke out in the bigger cities because people were hungry.

Bodybuilder, actor, and politician Arnold Schwarzenegger made it big when he played the muscle-bound Conan the Barbarian in the 1982 film of the same name.

His father may have been police chief, but Schwarzenegger grew up in a simple home in near poverty. He grew up without indoor plumbing, a refrigerator, or a telephone. Schwarzenegger's mother often went to farms asking for help to feed her family.[1]

Poverty wasn't the only problem in the Schwarzenegger household. Young Arnold felt that his father liked his older brother

Much of Germany and Austria was decimated during World War II. This photo of a street in Vienna, Austria, shows residents pulling their belongings on carts.

Meinhard better than him. And both of his parents were strict. They didn't hesitate to hit Arnold and his siblings for misbehaving. His father, however, did urge Arnold to play sports at a young age. The little boy was thin and quick, and he played soccer well.

Despite his tough childhood, Arnold was a happy, enthusiastic child in school who earned average grades. The highlight of his early years was when the family had saved enough money to afford a refrigerator.[2]

TRIP TO GYM CHANGES EVERYTHING

In 1960, Arnold's soccer coach took the team to a gym. There, Arnold touched his first barbell. He already admired bodybuilders and would see movies that featured some of his favorites, including Johnny Weissmuller, a bodybuilder who made a name for himself playing Tarzan in the movies.

So, when he stepped into the gym, Arnold fell in love with it. He liked the way his body felt after lifting weights, and he liked seeing his growing muscles. He soon stopped playing soccer to focus on weightlifting and bodybuilding.

This became a problem in his household. Arnold's parents feared that his love of bodybuilding meant that he was gay. He would tape posters of his favorite male bodybuilders above his bed, while his friends taped posters of girls to their walls. The difference made his parents uncomfortable. During this time period, many people felt homosexuality was unacceptable. Some people still have such views today.

Because of his bodybuilder posters, his very strict father would chase Arnold around and try to beat him. Arnold's mother even called a doctor to see if there was something that could be done to "cure" her son.

"I don't know if mum thought I was gay, or if she just thought there was something off. And 'let's catch it early,'" Schwarzenegger said during a 2016 interview. "She asked the doctor, 'Can you help me? I don't know if there's something wrong with my son because his wall is full of naked men. All of Arnold's friends have pictures of girls above their bed. And Arnold has no girls.'"[3]

Only a year later, when he was fourteen, Arnold knew what he wanted to do with his life. He wanted to be a professional bodybuilder and Olympic weightlifter. This led his parents to become more worried. His father wanted Arnold to follow in his footsteps and pursue a career in law enforcement. His mother kept urging him to go to trade school.[4]

But he held firm, telling his friends that he would one day live in the United States. He continued bodybuilding but knew strength alone would not help him fulfill his dreams. He realized that weight training was mental, or in the mind. He needed to overcome certain mental blocks, so he started training and studying psychology. He found out about a bodybuilder crowned Mr. Austria and became even more obsessed with the sport. Sometimes he would even break into the local gym on the weekends after it closed to fit in more workouts.

AUSTRIA

Austria, the birthplace of world-class athlete and movie star Arnold Schwarzenegger, is a landlocked, German-speaking country in central Europe. It is known for the beauty of the Alps.

It shares borders with several countries, including Germany, Switzerland, Italy, Czech Republic, Slovenia, Hungary, and Slovakia. During ancient times, Celtic tribes occupied the region but the Roman Empire eventually conquered them. After the fall of the Roman Empire, the Bavarians (from modern-day Germany) conquered the area. The German influence remains today.

(continued on the next page)

(continued from the previous page)

In the 1800s, Austria became a world power. It stands out for being one of the allied nations that put an end to France's aggression under Napoleon Bonaparte. As a result, the nation is credited for helping to end the Napoleonic Wars.

The mountainous nation has long been associated with Germany. At one point, it took on the name the Republic of German Austria. It also tried to become part of Germany. But treaties, or agreements, signed after World War I stopped Austria and German from uniting. The agreements aimed to prevent Germany from becoming a military superpower again. Those treaties, however, did not keep Germany from once again growing its army. And in 1938, as World War II began, Germany invaded Austria and made the country part of its territory. It remained part of Nazi Germany until the United States and its allies defeated Germany in 1945.

Today, Austria is a very modern country. As the twelfth richest nation in the world, it offers citizens a very high standard of living. Close to nine million people live there. In addition to Arnold Schwarzenegger, Austria has produced very famous and influential citizens. They include classical musician Wolfgang Amadeus Mozart and psychoanalyst Sigmund Freud. Psychoanalysts help patients treat problems with their personalities or minds.

This view of the Dachstein Mountains in Austria is just one of many gorgeous sights to see in the countryside.

MR. UNIVERSE

Schwarzenegger loved Hollywood films almost as much as he loved weightlifting, but his friends laughed when he told them he planned to move to the United States and become a big movie star.

In 1965, when he was eighteen years old, Schwarzenegger served a year in the Austrian army. The government required all male citizens to enlist, but by the time he completed his service, the relationship between Schwarzenegger and his family had grown cold. He never really recovered from the hurts of his early childhood.

He soon began winning bodybuilding contests in Austria and knew that could be his ticket out of the country and into stardom. He traveled to London to compete in the Mr. Universe contest and finished second. That's when he met Charles Bennett, a weightlifting coach who convinced Schwarzenegger to move in to his London home. Bennett and his family lived in a small apartment above one of the gyms he owned. He became Schwarzenegger's coach, mentor, and friend. In fact, the Bennett family sort of became Schwarzenegger's new family.

Both Charles Bennett and his wife, Diane, were bodybuilders. They helped Schwarzenegger with his English and his education, and they even gave him books to read. Before meeting them, he had never actually read a whole book!

"Being with them made me so much more sophisticated," Schwarzenegger told an English newspaper years later. "When you're the age I was then, you're always looking for approval, for love, for attention, and also for guidance. At the time, I wasn't really aware of that. But now, looking back, I see that the Bennett family fulfilled all those needs. They saw that I needed that care and attention and love."[5]

Schwarzenegger flexes his muscles in 1968 on a hilltop near the famous Muscle Beach in Santa Monica, California. His move to the state would help him become a movie star.

The Bennetts's guidance helped Schwarzenegger succeed. The following year, his dream came true when he won the title of Mr. Universe.

And, sure enough, his earlier prediction came true as well. Schwarzenegger received a contract to train in California and work for Joe Weider, a leader in the bodybuilding and weightlifting merchandise industry.

BOUND FOR CALIFORNIA

Schwarzenegger moved to the United States in 1968. Two years later, at the age of twenty-three, he won his first Mr. Olympia title. He would win four more by 1977, the same year that a bodybuilding documentary featured Schwarzenegger a great deal. Hollywood filmmakers took note of the handsome muscleman and thought they could use him in action movies.

In 1970, Schwarzenegger had appeared in a low-budget film called *Hercules in New York*. But his poor English and thick Austrian accent made it almost impossible for the audience to understand him. Producers ultimately dubbed another actor's voice over his. When *Pumping Iron* debuted in 1977, Schwarzenegger had already appeared in several small films and television shows, but nothing major. Meanwhile, he took English classes at the local community college and earned a business degree.

The hard work paid off, and in 1982 he won the title role in the box-office smash *Conan the Barbarian*. He acted in the film's sequel and became more well known. Playing Conan set him up for the part

The movie role Schwarzenegger may be best known for is the assassin robot from the future sent back in time to eliminate a possible threat in the 1984 blockbuster *The Terminator*.

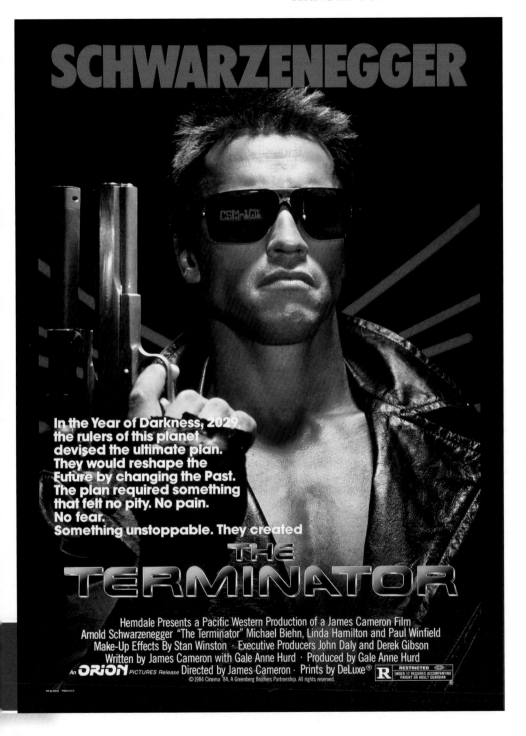

that would catapult him into Hollywood stardom. In 1984, he starred as a terrifying robot from the future in *The Terminator*, which made him known for the line "I'll be back."

Over the next few years, Schwarzenegger became Hollywood's leading action movie star. He followed up *The Terminator* with action hits such as *Commando, The Running Man, Last Action Hero,* and a *Terminator* sequel. He also became the highest-paid actor in Hollywood.

"My dream was to come to America, become the greatest bodybuilder of all time," he said in a newspaper interview. "And if all that worked out, I was going to build a gym business and then live happily ever after. Then all of a sudden I shot right by my dream. I stopped doing the strong man stuff, did the *Terminator* movies and became the highest-paid actor in Hollywood. I got $30 million for *Terminator 3*, you know."[6]

GIVING BACK

Arnold Schwarzenegger has never forgotten his difficult start in life. He has also never been shy about giving back and getting involved in charitable causes, especially if they involve children.

One cause has long been close to his heart—the Special Olympics. His ex-wife's mother, Eunice Kennedy Shriver, founded them. He even served as the official spokesman for the Special Olympics in 2007 when they took place in Shanghai, China.

Schwarzenegger has also worked on behalf of poor children who may not have the same educational and athletic opportunities

(continued on page 54)

Schwarzenegger has always had a soft spot in his heart for the Special Olympics, a program founded by his ex-wife's mother, Eunice Kennedy Shriver. Here, she attends a National Press Club lunch featuring Schwarzenegger as speaker in 2007.

(continued from page 54)

as their peers. In 1995, after establishing himself as a worldwide figure in several fields, Schwarzenegger helped introduce the Inner City Games, a foundation started in 1991 in Los Angeles, to the masses. The program strives to build the self-esteem of children from low-income urban areas. It also focuses on educational opportunities and academic excellence. Today, the program operates in several American cities.

In connection with the Inner City Games, Schwarzenegger began the After-School All-Stars (ASAS). The program gives students in inner cities a safe place to gather after school to do homework and play sports or games. The program emphasizes physical fitness, health, and nutrition.

One of the other charities and organizations Schwarzenegger has helped support over the years is Habitat for Humanity, which provides housing for the poor. He also participates in programs that fight human trafficking and slavery and help children affected by AIDS.

When he served as the governor of California, Schwarzenegger never accepted the $175,000 annual salary during his eight years in office. Instead, he told the state to donate the money to children's charities.

POLITICS

Schwarzenegger also proved that he could be funny by starring in comedic roles after playing leads in action films. He cracked audiences up in *Kindergarten Cop*, *Jingle All the Way*, and *Twins*.

Schwarzenegger and former wife, Maria Shriver, spent twenty-five years together as husband and wife. US president John F. Kennedy was Shriver's uncle.

In 1983, he became a naturalized US citizen. Three years later, when he wed Maria Shriver, he married into one of the most famous political families in the United States—the Kennedys. Shriver is the daughter of Eunice Kennedy Shriver, sister of President John F. Kennedy. Schwarzenegger's career turned to politics when he ran for governor of California in 2003.

He and Shriver separated after twenty-five years of marriage. Today, the man the *Los Angeles Times* once described as this country's most famous immigrant, continues to make movies and appear on television shows. He also offers his expertise to young bodybuilders.

CHAPTER 5

TAMBA HALI

T amba Hali is one of the few African-born players in the National Football League (NFL). Immigrating to the United States completely changed his life. The move gave him opportunities that he probably would have missed overseas.

A TOUGH BEGINNING

Tamba Hali was born November 3, 1983, in Gbarnga, Liberia, a country in West Africa. His mother raised him and his three siblings in a very poor part of Gbarnga. They lacked electricity and plumbing. They cooked meals outside because their small house was so hot. They took baths in a nearby stream. Life was simple, but that would soon change.

By the time, he was six years old, a bloody civil war had broken out in Liberia. Rebel soldiers tried to get boys as young as nine or ten years old to join them by scaring

Tamba Hali's rise from war-torn Liberia to the National Football League is an amazing story of survival and hard work. He is one of the league's greatest outside linebackers.

them or promising them food and shelter. They also gave the boys drugs and weapons. The soldiers often urged Tamba to join them by offering him a gun and food.[1] But his older brother protected him and told him to refuse to become a child soldier. The civil war marked a very dangerous time for Tamba and his siblings. People in their village died every day during the war.

LIBERIA

Liberia is one of the world's most unique countries. The West African country borders Sierra Leone, Guinea, and Ivory Coast. Its national language is English, but Liberia was never a British colony. Liberians speak English because its founders came from the United States.

Former slaves and other American blacks created Liberia in the early 1800s. Joseph Jenkins Roberts was the country's first president. He was a black man from Virginia, born a free man and not a slave.

Named after US president James Monroe, Monrovia is Liberia's capital city. The president supported the creation of an African colony for former slaves and their families. And Liberians modeled their country's constitution and declaration of independence after the American versions. Liberia helped the United States during World War II, and, in return, America poured money into Liberia to help the developing nation become more modern.

This 2012 photo of downtown Monrovia, Liberia, shows a bustling and thriving city. That has not always been the case. Liberia has seen its share of violence and bloodshed during civil wars and uprisings.

Since the 1980s, however, the country has suffered from economic and political instability stemming from civil war, poverty, military takeovers, and even deadly outbreaks of diseases like the Ebola virus. Liberia's civil wars alone caused five hundred thousand deaths, many of working adults and young people. The casualties have led to the country's economy to crumble.

NOWHERE TO GO

The brutal civil war left Liberia in shambles. After only a few years, it destroyed the roads and bridges. Survivors lived without electricity or running water and in constant chaos.

To make matters worse, a vicious warlord named Charles Taylor made Gbarnga his headquarters. Taylor led the rebels who tried to overthrow the government. With no schools and no police in the area, the city had no law and order.

Years before, Tamba's father, Henry, fled the country for the United States. He promised to send his children to America, where they could live in safety. Educated by Christian missionaries, Henry Hali earned a degree at the local college near Gbarnga. He worked as a teacher and then as a college professor before escaping to the United States, where he taught at New Jersey's Fairleigh Dickinson University. He planned to become a US citizen to help bring his children to the country.

But the fighting became worse and Tamba's mother, Rachel Keita, decided to leave Gbarnga. It was a dangerous move, but she took her children to the countryside where they lived in the forest and ate whatever they could find, like cassava roots and other wild vegetables.[2]

On one occasion, the family traveled to another region on the back of a truck. They passed many checkpoints manned by soldiers, many not much older than Tamba himself. At one checkpoint, the soldiers fired their guns. Tamba stood up and yelled at them to stop, but his older brother grabbed him and pulled him down to safety.[3]

In 1992, the fighting lessened, and other countries sent in soldiers to maintain the peace. Tamba's mother decided to leave the

Warlord and rebel leader Charles Taylor holds a press conference in 1990, moments before going on the radio and claiming victory against the government's forces.

forest and return her family to their village. But before long, the family saw government planes shoot and drop bombs on people they believed were rebel soldiers. They did not realize they were villagers.

Living in terror became a daily occurrence. People ran and hid when they heard planes overhead. Tamba's mother decided her family deserved more. She sought a permanent refuge, a new home, for them. She took her children on a half-day's drive to the Ivory Coast, a neighboring country.

When they reached the border, the soldiers refused to let anyone through. But Tamba's older brother, who had helped Taylor's forces by operating a shortwave radio, convinced the soldiers to allow his family to cross. At long last, the family escaped war-torn Liberia.[4]

SAFE AT LAST

After Tamba Hali settled in the Ivory Coast, his father visited for the first time in years. He gained visas (travel papers) for all of his children to go to the United States. The children left the Ivory Coast, but without their mother. At age eleven and skinny with glasses, Tamba Hali tried to adjust to life in a strange, new land.

He grew quickly in his new country. In eighth grade, Tamba was 6 feet tall (183 cm) and 160 pounds (72.5 kilograms). A teacher took notice and called the football coach at Teaneck High School in New Jersey. Together, the coach and the teacher convinced Tamba to play football in the ninth grade. Once in high school, he struggled to memorize the plays and understand strategy. By his sophomore season, though, football made more sense. In twelfth grade, Tamba was the best player on the team and almost every major college in the country tried to recruit him. Tamba chose Penn State University, where he played under coach Joe Paterno. He became one of the greatest defensive ends in college football.

WHY PENN STATE IS NICKNAMED "LINEBACKER U"

Penn State University has long been a football powerhouse. Many of the school's players have become NFL linebackers. For that reason, some people call it "Linebacker U" or "Linebacker University."

Penn State linebackers who went on to achieve stardom in the NFL include Tamba Hali, Jack Ham, Lavar Arrington, Cameron Wake, Sean Lee, and NaVorro Bowman. The tradition started in 1967 when the first of many All-American linebackers thrived under Joe Paterno's coaching. Dennis Onkotz, who played middle linebacker for the Nittany Lions, was one of Penn State's first great linebackers.

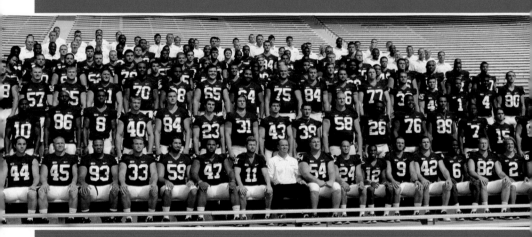

Hali had a great college career at "Linebacker University," otherwise known as Penn State. This is a team photo of the 2012 squad. The school continues to pump out great NFL linebackers.

(continued on the next page)

(continued from the previous page)

A fierce hitter and run-stopper, Onkotz also had track speed and previously played safety. This meant he was faster and more athletic than a traditional linebacker. He was so athletic that the coaching staff made him the team's punt returner, a spot usually reserved for a slender speedster, not a bruising linebacker.

But athleticism alone didn't separate Penn State linebackers from the rest. They also made big plays. The school's linebackers regularly recovered fumbles and made interceptions to save games.

For example, when Penn State played Illinois in 1999, linebacker Lavar Arrington anticipated the snap count on fourth down and dove headfirst over the offensive tackle to bring down the running back in the backfield. The move gave Penn State the ball. It's now known as the "Lavar Leap."

REUNION WITH HIS MOTHER

While he played football in college, Hali also studied hard to earn a degree in broadcast journalism. In addition, he prepared to become an American citizen and worked with Paterno's lawyer brother to move his mother out of West Africa and into the United States. His mother suffered a gunshot wound after being caught in civil war violence. She had other health problems as well.

When the Kansas City Chiefs chose Hali in the first round of the 2006 NFL draft, he became an American citizen and moved his mother to the United States. "My mum was in my life from day one. So having her here after being away from her for 12 years … it was a situation almost like your parent was dead for 12 years and now she's back in your life," he said.[5]

Reuniting with his mother wasn't Hali's only accomplishment. He became an NFL superstar with the Chiefs. During his first eleven seasons with the team, Hali made the Pro Bowl five times. The event is reserved for the season's best players. Plus, he is closing in on one hundred career quarterback sacks, has forced thirty-two fumbles, and intercepted two passes. He is the second all-time sack leader in Chiefs history behind the legendary Derrick Thomas.

Hali's durability is also impressive. He has missed only two games in eleven seasons. But in 2016, the big defensive player did show signs of slowing down. The Chiefs rested him often in games because of his aching knees. Many people thought Hali's knees would keep him off the field in 2016, but they were wrong.

"When I hit the field, I go," Hali said. "Whether my knee's hurting or not, as long as I'm on the field and I can run, I go. I think the coaches understand that."[6]

Hali, who eats his mother's cooking most nights, also played in 2017. In his spare time, he likes to write rap music and practice Brazilian martial arts. He also donates much of his money to Liberian issues. The country continues to heal from decades of violence and bad blood.

He has yet to return there since moving to the United States at age eleven, but he doesn't rule out visiting after his football days are over. "Plus we have work to do here. When time permits, I think I'll go back. Right now I want to finish what we've started here."[7]

Hali has said he's concerned about violence in Liberia. His fears make sense. He likely has few good memories of home.

CHAPTER 6

MARIA SHARAPOVA

The comeback of Russian-born tennis sensation Maria Sharapova will be just as interesting to watch as her rise, which stunned the tennis world and catapulted her into the top one hundred female tennis players of all time.

Maria Yuryevna Sharapova was born on April 19, 1987, in Nyagan, Russia, to Yuri and Yelena Sharapova. Because the family lived in Belarus, very close to where the Chernobyl nuclear disaster occurred a year earlier, the family fled the area. They feared the nuclear fallout and radioactivity would make them sick. They moved to Siberia, where Yuri found work on the oil pipelines.

A NATURAL

A cyclist and skier, Maria's father was very athletic. He thought he was good enough to become a professional in either sport but never did. One day, as he knocked a tennis ball on a pockmarked and rutted tennis court with his three-year-old daughter, he noticed her excellent coordination.[1]

Yuri knew his daughter had a gift. Despite her extremely young age, she could hit a tennis ball over the net. He knew that to feed that talent he would have to leave Siberia for a warmer place with better tennis

Russian-born Maria Sharapova holds the award for winning the 2004 Wimbledon Ladies' Singles championship.

facilities. So, the family moved to Sochi, which is very close to the Black Sea. There, the climate is better suited for tennis.

"If Chernobyl had never happened, my life would have been very different," Sharapova would say years later. "I probably wouldn't even be playing tennis. It's crazy to think I could have been born in the midst of all that. I remember my mom and dad saying that it was chaos. So I'm extremely lucky that I got out of it. There are 'what ifs?' What if I was never a tennis player?"[2]

CHERNOBYL

The name of the Russian city Chernobyl has become synonymous with disaster, specifically nuclear disaster. The Chernobyl disaster refers to the April 26, 1986, accident at the Chernobyl nuclear plant. The accident happened because safety measures were ignored during a late-night stress test of operations. The test caused a sudden and unexpected power surge. When workers attempted to use emergency shutdown procedures, somehow even more power was produced, causing a massive fire.

Giant plumes of fire and smoke shot from the power plant, sending massive amounts of radioactive fallout into the sky and the surrounding areas. Most of the radioactive fallout landed in Belarus. Surrounding areas were evacuated, but the winds made it difficult to decide where to send evacuees to safety. The breezes made the radioactivity travel.

Thirty-one workers at the plant died almost immediately, and officials predicted that the radioactivity would later lead to nearly five hundred cancer deaths. The contaminated land near the power plant has been abandoned since the accident, an eerie

(continued on page 70)

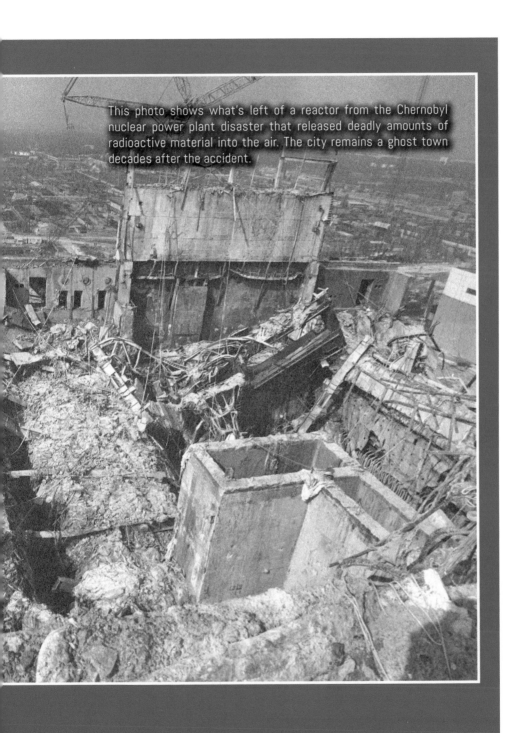

This photo shows what's left of a reactor from the Chernobyl nuclear power plant disaster that released deadly amounts of radioactive material into the air. The city remains a ghost town decades after the accident.

(continued from page 68)

sight that includes houses, schools, and amusement parks in good condition. Yet, they remain unused and empty. Everything—including the ground, trees and water—is considered contaminated to this day.

The International Atomic Energy Commission found that the Chernobyl accident released 400 percent more radioactive material into the air than the atomic bomb the United States dropped on Hiroshima, Japan, during World War II.

SOCHI

In Sochi, Maria's father became friends with a man whose son (Yevgeny Kafelnikof) would go on to win a couple of major tennis tournaments. She soon began practicing with her father on a regular basis at a local park. Because Sochi is a resort town, tennis courts tended to get very crowded. So Sharapova and her dad would take a 5 a.m. bus to get to the tennis courts before the tourists arrived. Then they would play all day.[3]

When her father realized that he could no longer coach her because of her exceptional talent, he hired a coach named Yuri Yutkin to help her get even better. The coach found the young girl impressive. In 1993, when she was six years old, Maria took part in a tennis clinic in Moscow that Czech tennis legend Martina Navratilova organized. Navratilova took one look at the girl and told Yuri to take Maria to Bradenton, Florida, home of the world's best tennis schools and professional coaches. She specifically recommended the IMG

Academy, where tennis greats such as Andre Agassi, Monica Seles, and Anna Kournikova trained as youngsters.

Yuri saved as much money as he could and applied for a scholarship for his daughter. Unfortunately, immigration rules prevented Maria's mother from traveling as well. This resulted in Maria living apart from her mother for the next several years. The arrangement could have destroyed a family.

Maria had a tough time adjusting. Some of the other girls made fun of her accent. They also made fun of her father, who worked as a restaurant dishwasher to help support his daughter. But Yuri made sure that his daughter practiced all the time. Sometimes she practiced so hard that blisters formed on her hands.[4]

She eventually won a full scholarship and trained in Bradenton for the next several years, learning both tennis and English. Just about anyone who saw her play knew that she had the potential for greatness. For the next several years, she trained to become stronger and faster and to perfect her form on the tennis court. She also performed lots of exercises to improve her already amazing hand-eye coordination.

TIME TO WIN

In 2000, when she was only thirteen years old, Maria won her first international tournament for juniors. She managed to win even though she'd competed against girls who were sixteen years old with more experience than she had. She also won the Rising Star Award for the best young player in the tournament with the most promise. A year later, she made it to the finals of the junior Wimbledon and Australian Open tournaments. With a junior record of 47–9, Maria ranked sixth among the world's junior tennis players by the end of 2002.

Among Sharapova's biggest rivals on the tennis court have been the amazing Williams sisters. Venus and Serena Williams have dominated the winner's podium, along with Sharapova.

The time had come for Maria to leave the junior circuit and play professionally. In 2003, she struggled against the older and more experienced players in some of the bigger tournaments. She lost in the first round of the French and Australian opens but excelled in smaller tournaments. She won the Japan Open Tennis Championship and the Bell Challenge. For her efforts, the Women's Tennis Association named her newcomer of the year.

The next year would be one for the ages. She advanced in some of the early majors and won a small tournament before jetting off to London for Wimbledon. Two American sisters, Venus and Serena Williams, had dominated Wimbledon for four years, making the championship a family affair, so Maria only aimed to improve on her performance from the previous year.

STUNNING UPSET

The seventeen-year-old won a series of matches that earned her a great deal of media attention during Wimbledon. The public flocked to watch her play and root for her to win. Sharapova played her way into the finals, but

MELDONIUM

How did Maria Sharapova get her hands on Meldonium? The medication is not licensed or available in the United States. However, it is available and legal in Russia, Sharapova's birthplace, which she still represents during international competitions.

The drug, which enhances a person's oxygen intake, can treat irregular heartbeats, mild heart conditions, and early stages of diabetes. The drugmaker maintains that the drug does not enhance athletic performance. But because the World Anti-Doping Agency includes Meldonium on its list of banned substances, professional tennis players may not take it.

Sharapova said that she had taken the drug for ten years before its addition to the list of banned substances. She explained that her doctor had prescribed the drug in 2006 to treat her health problems, including a magnesium deficiency and an irregular heartbeat. Sharapova also said that when her doctor first prescribed the drug, it was not called Meldonium. In light of this information, officials reduced her suspension from two years to fifteen months.

Latvian scientist Ivars Kalvins, Meldonium's inventor, objects to the Anti-Doping Agency banning the drug. He said the ban would be harmful to athletes who need the drug to protect their hearts while competing.

"Make no mistake, the number of deaths among athletes on the pitch will be growing. Who will answer for this? Not WADA (World Anti-Doping Agency)—they'll shrug it off," he said. "This will mean that the athletes themselves are to blame for crossing the line."[7]

Sharapova was suspended from playing tennis professionally after officials discovered that she had been taking the banned drug Meldonium. It is legal and not banned in Russia.

it seemed doubtful that she would come out on top. She had to square off against Serena Williams, one of the best tennis players in the world. In fact, Williams had won Wimbledon the previous two years.

But in a shocking display of domination, Sharapova was quicker, stronger, and more exact with her shots and volleys than Williams. The match took only seventy-three minutes, and when Williams's final shot went into the net, Sharapova fell to her knees and covered her face in joy and disbelief. She ran into the stands where she hugged her father, who smothered her with kisses.[5]

Then, as officials waited at center court to award her the Silver Cup and a very large check, Sharapova asked for a cell phone. She repeatedly tried to reach her mother in Florida, but the calls kept dropping. Finally, she thanked her parents while accepting her awards, telling them they had made her a winner. Afterward, reporters asked the giggling, emotional teenager about her strategy and tactics. How had she beaten the best player in the world?

"To tell you the truth, I don't know what happened in the match," Sharapova said with a high-pitched laugh. "I don't know how I won. I don't know what the tactics were. I was just playing. I was in my own little world."[6]

Williams would get her revenge the following year during a very close match at the Australian Open. But it didn't matter. "Maria-Mania" was real, and everywhere she played, fans flocked to see her. Of course, it didn't hurt that she kept winning tournaments. In 2005, she briefly became the top-ranked female tennis player in the world. The next year, she added another Grand Slam victory to her résumé by winning the US Open.

DOMINANCE

For the next decade, Sharapova continued to be one of the best tennis players in the world. But shoulder injuries slowed her down, and she found herself in a scandal in 2016. Officials suspended her from play for more than a year because she tested positive for a banned drug called Meldonium. The news crushed Sharapova, who lost numerous endorsement deals and fans who now viewed her as a cheat.

Before the Meldonium scandal, Sharapova considered retiring from tennis because she'd been slowing down. But afterward, she was determined to return to tennis better than ever in 2017. She trained non-stop for the first four months of the year to make sure her reflexes would be sharp upon her April return. She did not want a controversial suspension to end her career.

"You always want to end your career or a chapter in your life on your terms and in your voice," Sharapova said. "And to be in a moment where you felt like it could have ended on someone else's terms was very difficult for me to accept. That's why I fought so hard for the truth to be out. You don't realize how much you love something, how much something means to you, until you lose it for some time."[8]

CHAPTER 7

PATRICK EWING

Who knew Patrick Ewing would grow up to be a professional basketball player? The athlete was twelve years old before he'd even seen a basketball or knew anything about the sport. Despite his delayed introduction to the game, Patrick Ewing became a legendary professional basketball player and Hall of Fame inductee.

Patrick Aloysius Ewing was born August 5, 1962, in Kingston, Jamaica, to Carl and Dorothy Ewing. His father worked as an auto mechanic, and his mother stayed home to raise Patrick and his six brothers and sisters. With very little money to go around, his childhood was tough. The family home on Bond Street sat in the poorest part of the city.

A MOTHER'S DECISION

The crime and poverty in Jamaica's capital city was oppressive, and that worried Patrick's mother. She wanted her children to have a better life than she and her husband had. She knew few opportunities awaited her children in Jamaica, so she decided to do something drastic.

She left the country. She landed a job as a hospital worker in Massachusetts and planned to save enough money to allow her husband and children to join

No member of the New York Knicks will ever wear the number thirty-three jersey again. It belonged to longtime all-star Patrick Ewing, and the Knicks retired his jersey after Ewing stopped playing professionally.

her in the United States. In 1971, she began moving her family from Kingston, Jamaica, to Cambridge, Massachusetts.

But Carl Ewing hesitated to leave his job and country, and Patrick felt nervous about leaving behind everyone and everything he knew. "At first, it was a change. I was sad because I was leaving my friends," he said. "But life goes on. You have to make new friends and go on. I felt very comfortable. After all, this was my very first home."[1]

In Jamaica, basketball was hardly the most popular sport. Cricket, soccer, track and field, and a women's sport called netball all ranked higher in popularity than basketball. But when Patrick walked by a Cambridge playground and saw kids his age playing basketball in the park, he took an interest. One of the kids invited Patrick to join in, and he was hooked.[2]

BASKETBALL?

When Patrick first stepped onto the basketball court, some of the kids laughed because he knew practically nothing about the game he enjoyed so much. "I never knew what basketball was," Ewing said. "I started playing on the playground. People used to laugh at me and joke at me because I was so tall, and I didn't know the game and I couldn't play it."[3]

Patrick attended Cambridge Rindge and Latin School, which provided scholarships for poor families. Because of his interest in playing basketball and his growing height, Patrick caught the attention of coach John Fountain. He helped Patrick understand the game and get better at it.

Soon, Patrick became a high school star, which exposed him to racism. "When I first came to Boston, no question about that," he said. "Racism is everywhere, whether it's whites against blacks or Jews versus Catholics. It's in Jamaica. It's sad. After all these years, it's still there and something everyone still has to work on."[4]

JAMAICA

The island nation of Jamaica is located in the Caribbean Ocean about 90 miles (145 km) south of Cuba and 120 miles (193 km) west of Hispaniola—the island that houses both the Dominican Republic and Haiti. As he had with much of the Caribbean, Christopher Columbus also explored Jamaica. The Spaniards settled there as well, exposing the natives to deadly diseases. The Spanish also brought enslaved Africans to Jamaica.

Spain controlled the island from 1494 to 1655, when the English took control. England made a profit from Jamaica by turning the country into a large exporter of sugar. The country remained an English colony until 1962, when Jamaica won its independence. The third largest island in the Caribbean, Jamaica contains beautiful beaches, forests, mountains, and waterfalls.

The island is 92 percent black. The birthplace of reggae musician Bob Marley, Jamaica is a popular tourist destination. A large portion of the population lives in poverty, however.

A number of world-class athletes come from Jamaica, especially in track and field, an area in which Usain Bolt has broken multiple records for sprinting. Four former track stars formed the now-famous Jamaican bobsled team, which competed in the 1982 Olympics. It marked the first time a nation without snowfall qualified in the sport. They have now competed in the Olympics several times since and are normally fan favorites.

Racists called Patrick the N-word and prevented him from visiting certain neighborhoods. Opposing teams often rocked his bus during basketball games. But Patrick grew to be 7 feet (213 cm) tall and strong. He was a powerful defensive player and eventually a scorer. Every university wanted Patrick to play for them after high school.

RACISM SHAPES HIS FUTURE

Racism determined which school Ewing chose. The University of North Carolina had one of the best programs in the country, but when coach Dean Smith brought Ewing to visit the campus, the young athlete decided not to attend the school.

"I was close [to attending UNC]. North Carolina was a very good school but, you know, when I went down there they put me in that Carolina Inn, and there was a big Ku Klux Klan rally at North Carolina when I was there," Ewing said. "And I'm like, 'You know what? I'm not coming down here.'"[5]

Instead, he accepted a scholarship to Georgetown University, home of African American head basketball coach John Thompson. Thompson's presence made Ewing feel comfortable. He became a starter for the basketball team freshman year. He led the team to the finals, but Georgetown lost the championship to North Carolina.

In 1984, the following year, Ewing helped the Georgetown Hoyas defeat the University of Houston to win the NCAA title. He returned the team to the finals the next season, but they fell to Villanova. While at Georgetown, the basketball star became a US citizen.

Ewing hugs legendary coach and mentor John Thompson during one of Georgetown University's college basketball games. The school is known for producing great centers such as Ewing, Alonzo Mourning, and Dikembe Mutombo.

NBA SUPERSTAR

A college basketball standout, Ewing was the first player chosen in the 1985 NBA draft. He ended up on the New York Knicks. During his first year in the NBA, Ewing suffered a few nagging injuries but still managed to win the NBA Rookie of the Year Award. He'd averaged twenty points, nine rebounds, and two blocked shots per game. The rest of the Knicks performed poorly, but Ewing gave the Big Apple hope that the team would improve.

After his rookie season, the Jamaican government flew Ewing and his family to the island to honor him during a special celebration. The Knicks eventually hired head coach Pat Riley, and he built a very strong team around Ewing's strengths of rebounding, blocking shots, and defending the rim. The Knicks repeatedly made the play-offs, and Ewing made the NBA All-Star team eleven times. He also belonged to the gold medal–winning Olympic Dream Team that crushed the competition in 1992. And that's not all. Ewing made the list of the top fifty greatest players in NBA history.

SEARCHING FOR A CHAMPIONSHIP

Known for his fire and tenacity on the court, Patrick Ewing regretted that he never led the Knicks to the championship that the team and New York City desperately wanted. Early in his career, he faced criticism for not sharing the details of his private life, but he said his sole focus was to win a championship.

"I like who I am, and I'm very comfortable with the way I am," Ewing told the *New York Times*. "I'm a laid-back, normal-type person. There are other guys who always want the spotlight, but not me. I can

THE NBA'S TOP 50 PLAYERS

The NBA celebrated its fiftieth anniversary in 1997 at the All-Star Game in Cleveland. During halftime, the lights dimmed and dramatic music sounded. The crowd rose to their feet expecting something amazing to happen. One-by-one, forty-seven of the greatest fifty NBA players to step on the hardwood appeared on the court. The NBA polled journalists, former players, coaches, and current and former general managers to create a list of the fifty best NBA players ever.

Some of the players had long ago retired. Some had only recently retired, and eleven were active players. They included Charles Barkley, Clyde Drexler, Michael Jordan, Karl Malone, Shaquille O'Neal, Hakeem Olajuwon, Robert Parish, Scottie Pippen, David Robinson, John Stockton, and, of course, Patrick Ewing.

Ewing was honored to make the list and promised to keep working hard. ESPN had previously named him the sixteenth greatest college player of all time.

do without all that. I just want to win a championship. My career will be somewhat unfulfilled, in my mind, until I win one."[6]

Ewing came close to winning a championship a few times. He led the team to the NBA Finals against the Houston Rockets in 1992 and then against the San Antonio Spurs in 1998. Unfortunately, an injury prevented him from playing in the 1998 finals.

Today, Ewing lives in New Jersey. He has three children, including a son, Patrick Ewing Jr., who plays basketball professionally in Europe. He has several endorsement deals and his own athletics line that includes basketball sneakers.

Ewing remains very involved in the sport. After his playing days ended, he began coaching. He has served as an assistant coach with the Houston Rockets, Orlando Magic, and Charlotte Bobcats. He hopes to become an NBA head coach. He has yet to get the opportunity. Every time a head-coaching job opens up in New York, Knicks fans hope he will return to the team and lead them to the championship he missed out on as a player.

CHAPTER 8

MARIANO RIVERA

Mariano Rivera may be the best relief pitcher to ever play baseball. He was born in Panama City, Panama, on November 29, 1969. The second-born child of Mariano Rivera Palacios and Della Jiron, the baseball star has one older sister and two younger brothers.

BASEBALL AND FISH

The Riveras lived in a small fishing village called Puerto Caimito, where Mariano's father was a fishing boat captain. Mariano spent his free time playing soccer on the beach with friends. He adored Brazilian soccer superstar Pelé.

But sometimes Mariano played baseball, too. He soon discovered that he played baseball better than other sports. His friends later recalled how much he hated

A very relaxed Mariano Rivera visits old friends during a trip to Yankee Stadium after he retired as the greatest relief pitcher in the game's history.

87

Brazilian soccer legend Pelé, wearing the gold jersey, is considered by many to be the greatest soccer player of all time.

to lose. Sometimes he would get upset and toss the baseball into the ocean, declaring that the game ended in a tie.[1]

Mariano and his friends couldn't play baseball anytime they liked. Living in a seaside village meant the tides controlled everyone's plans. When it was high tide, the men in Puerto Caimito had their sons help them get their fishing boats in the water. Low tide meant there was plenty of room on the sand to go out and play baseball, but the conditions weren't perfect. The seashells often cut the boys' feet as they chased the ball. Sometimes the kids accidentally hit baseballs into the ocean, so they practiced hitting the balls straight to avoid losing them.[2]

As a teen, Mariano joined a few different baseball teams and excelled. But his family did not intend for him to become a professional baseball player. Instead, they expected him to work on a fishing boat as his father and other relatives had. But the work was dangerous. Mariano's uncle Miguel died from his injuries during a boating accident. The danger of the work led Mariano to consider a baseball career.

"From that moment, I think he became fearful," his father said. "From then on he began to practice more and go to the stadium."[3]

PANAMA

The Republic of Panama is a Central American country (sometimes labeled North American) that borders Colombia, Costa Rica, the Caribbean Sea, and the Pacific Ocean. The Spaniards conquered Panama in the sixteenth century, and the country remained a colony until 1821, when Colombia took control of it. With the help of the United States, Panama broke away from Colombia in 1903. This allowed the United States to send in the Army Corps of Engineers to build the Panama Canal, which lets ships go from the Caribbean to the Pacific and vice versa.

The mountain-filled nation has enjoyed more than twenty years of growth and stability since American forces went in and arrested Panamanian dictator Manuel Noriega, who terrorized the nation for decades with his harsh rule and ties to Colombian drug lords. The country has an unemployment rate of less than 3 percent, according to the CIA

(continued on page 92)

Fishing is a big industry for Panama, and it is how many people in the country make their living. This is a typical fishing village. Note how the houses sit on stilts above the water.

(continued from page 92)

Factbook. This means almost everyone in the country has work. But while the middle class continues to grow, a huge gap exists between the middle class and the very poor. More than 25 percent of the population lives in poverty.

In recent years, the country's tourism industry has grown. Many Americans and other foreigners retire in Panama because of its healthy economy and tax laws. Mariano Rivera is not the only great baseball player from the country. Rod Carew and Carlos Lee were born there, as was boxer Roberto Duran.

FROM SHORTSTOP TO PITCHER

The region where Rivera grew up produced a few minor league baseball players but no major stars. Still, many teams had scouts in the area looking for new talent. Just two years after he watched his uncle die in a boating accident, Rivera's baseball career picked up. A New York Yankees scout spotted Rivera as he played shortstop. The scout liked his athleticism but didn't think he would be able to hit major league pitching. But the following year, Rivera switched to pitching and performed during an open tryout for the Yankees. The same scout noticed him again and signed the twenty-year-old to a minor league contract with a bonus of $2,500.

In 1990, Rivera left his home in Panama for the Yankees' Gulf Coast League team in Florida. There, he excelled as a relief pitcher. Still, no one in the organization expected him to make it to the big leagues. Also, Rivera missed home and struggled to learn English. He spent most of his free time writing letters to his loved ones in Panama. He couldn't call them because no one in his family had a phone.

On the final day of the season, Rivera's manager asked him to start because the young pitcher could earn an extra $500 if he won the earned run title. But he needed a few more innings. Rivera threw a no-hitter for seven innings and suddenly everyone in the Yankees organization took notice.[4]

With no Spanish speakers on his team the next year, Rivera forced himself to learn English. He later became a mentor to many young Spanish-speaking players.

INCREDIBLE COMMAND

Rivera's talent impressed the Yankees organization. Coaches and talent evaluators especially liked his strikeout-to-walk ratio, or the number of strikeouts a pitcher has compared to the number of walks he gives. In 1991, for example, Rivera struck out 123 batters and walked only 36 in the minor leagues.

Rivera experienced success in his personal life that year also. He married his childhood sweetheart, Clara, and they later had three children. Rivera planned to raise his family in Panama.[5] But by 2000, the family had settled in Westchester County, New York, where they still live. And in 2015, Rivera became a US citizen.

Rivera had incredible command of his pitches, including one that right-handed batters struggled to handle. Called a "cutter," the pitch would rise up and in on them at the last second. In 1995, after five years of rising through the minor leagues, Rivera received a chance to start for the Yankees. The team contacted him because one of their pitchers was hurt. Unfortunately, Rivera's debut was terrible. He allowed five runs in only a few innings, and the Yankees lost 10–0. He played horribly in his next few starts, so the Yankees sent him back to the minor leagues.

Rivera celebrates with his family after being named the most valuable player at the 2013 Major League Baseball All-Star Game at Citi Field in New York.

There, he relied on his strong religious faith to keep his spirits high. He credits God with helping him speed up his pitches from the mid- to late 90s. Suddenly, he could throw pitches at 97 and 98 miles (156–157 km) per hour. He pitched so well in the minors that the Yankees contacted him again. He did well as a starter, but the Yankees moved him into a relief role as they prepared for the play-offs. Rivera was outstanding, and the Yankees decided to keep him there.

In 1996, he served as the set-up man for the team's closer, John Wetteland, and he helped the Yankees win the World Series. The set-up man normally pitches the eighth inning and holds onto the lead before turning the ball over to the closer. The following year, the Yankees decided not to keep Wetteland, and they named Rivera the team's closer.

FROM SETUP TO CLOSER

Some people criticized the Yankees for letting Wetteland go, but the decision allowed Mariano Rivera to become the greatest closer in baseball. His strategy was simple: don't overthink things and treat the batter as the enemy. He said that overthinking could cause a pitcher to get emotional and make mistakes.

"Go after hitters. When they're in the batter's box, they're the enemy. If you give them a chance, they'll kill you," he said. "Don't let them breathe. Never get beat with your second-best pitch. Play hard. God gave me this talent, so I use it."[6]

CLOSERS

The role of the baseball closer has changed a lot throughout baseball history. Even the term "closer" has changed. The relief pitchers teams used during jams were once called "firemen." In the 1970s, Major League Baseball even gave out an annual award for Fireman of the Year.

During baseball's early days in the late 1890s and through its golden era, most starting pitchers were expected to go the distance and throw complete games. Managers only went to their bullpen for a relief pitcher if an injury occurred or the starting pitcher became ineffective. In fact, some starting pitchers would even pitch both games of a doubleheader!

As Major League Baseball poured more money into starting pitchers and took great care to protect their arms and prolong their careers, the relief pitcher's role changed. Now good closers are among the highest-paid and sought-after players in the game. Today, starting pitchers are rarely expected to go past six innings. Teams use middle relievers, set-up men, and even lefty specialists before they bring in their closer to record the last three outs of the game and secure the victory.

In the past, closers or firemen often pitched more than one inning, sometimes going as many as three or four innings in relief. Now it's surprising when closers get more than three outs. When a closer is brought in to get a four-out save, it's a big deal. That means the reliever was brought in to record the final out of the eighth inning and the three outs in the ninth.

The fans nicknamed Rivera "Mo" and "Sandman" because he liked to take the pitcher's mound to the Metallica song "Enter Sandman." As a Yankee in the late 1990s and 2000s, he saw the team win five World Series championships. When Rivera retired in 2013 with 652 saves, he was baseball's greatest all-time saves leader. He finished 952 games and nine seasons with at least 40 saves, both records. He made the American All-Star team thirteen times, won six Reliever of the Year awards, and was also a World Series MVP. Major League Baseball has since named the Reliever of the Year Award after him.

Of course, Rivera earned an enormous amount of praise during his career, including from former Minnesota Twins manager Tom Kelly. After watching Rivera pitch nine straight innings of relief without allowing one hit, Kelly said, "He needs to pitch in a higher league, if there is one. Ban him from baseball. He should be illegal."[7]

And when the athlete wasn't playing baseball, he still managed to impress. Rivera spent many of his off-seasons doing mission work for the poor in Panama and other developing nations. He has donated money to build schools, churches, and medical clinics. In 2014, Rivera received two prestigious awards for his charity work. He won the Jackie Robinson Foundation's ROBIE Humanitarian Award and the Jefferson Award for Public Service.

Rivera now runs a church in Westchester County, New York, where his wife is pastor.

CHAPTER NOTES

INTRODUCTION

1. "Major League Baseball Players by Birthplace During the 2016 Season," Baseball-Almanac.com, http://www.baseball-almanac.com/players/birthplace.php?y=2016.
2. "Major League Baseball Players by Birthplace During the 1920 Season," Baseball-Almanac.com, http://www.baseball-almanac.com/players/birthplace.php?y=1920.
3. Sandra Harwitt, "Young American Tennis Players Share Immigrant Roots," *USA Today*, January 15, 2017, http://www.usatoday.com/story/sports/tennis/2017/01/15/frances-tiafoe-michael-mmoh-stefan-kozlov/96613080/.

CHAPTER 1: DIKEMBE MUTOMBO

1. Heidi Frontani, "Success Story for DRC: Dikembe Mutombo, a Most Generous Athlete," African Development Success, December 7, 2014, https://africandevelopmentsuccesses.wordpress.com/2014/12/07/success-story-from-the-drc-dikembe-mutombo-a-most-generous-athlete/.
2. "Dikembe Mutombo: Growing Up in Africa," Sports.Jrank.org, http://sports.jrank.org/pages/3382/Mutombo-Dikembe-Growing-Up-in-Africa.html.
3. Heidi Frontani, "Success Story for DRC: Dikembe Mutombo, a Most Generous Athlete."
4. "Dikembe Mutombo: Growing Up in Africa."
5. Michael Lee, "Dikembe Mutombo: A Hall of Fame Player with a Global Reach," *Washington Post*, Sept. 10, 2015, https://www.washingtonpost.com/news/sports/wp/2015/09/10/dikembe-mutombo-a-hall-of-fame-player-with-global-reach/?utm_term=.f3974b97faca
6. Ibid.

7. Christopher Dempsey, "Bickerstaff: 'Only Regret' as Nuggets GM Was Not Re-signing Mutombo," *Denver Post*, Sept. 11, 2015, http://blogs.denverpost.com/nuggets/2015/09/11/bickerstaff-only-regret-as-nuggets-gm-was-not-re-signing-mutombo/13292/.

8. George W. Bush, "President Bush Delivers State of the Union Address," whitehouse.gov, Jan. 23, 2007, https://georgewbush-whitehouse.archives.gov/stateoftheunion/2007/.

9. "Dikembe Mutombo Stands Tall with Bush (video)," AfricaHit.com, January 24, 2007, http://www.africahit.com/news/article/othersenglish/1162/?highlight=Dikembe+Mutombo&match=.

CHAPTER 2: ALBERT PUJOLS

1. Rob Rains, *Albert the Great: The Albert Pujols Story*, Champaign, IL: Sports Publishing LLC, 2005.

2. Daniel Woodman, "All-Star Pujols Anchored by Faith," *Baptist Press*, July 14, 2015, http://www.bpnews.net/45136/allstar-pujols-anchored-by-faith.

3. Joe Posnanski, "The Power to Believe," *Sports Illustrated*, March 16, 2009, http://www.si.com/vault/2009/03/16/105787315/the-power-to-believe.

4. Daniel Woodman, "All-Star Pujols Anchored by Faith."

5. Joe Posnanski, "The Power to Believe."

6. Arne Christensen, "Albert Pujols: Revisiting the Early Years," Hardball Times, June 15, 2010, http://www.hardballtimes.com/albert-pujols-revisiting-the-early-years/.

7. "A Look at Albert Pujols' Perfect Swing," *USA Today*, Feb. 23, 2011, http://usatoday30.usatoday.com/sports/baseball/nl/cardinals/albert-pujols-swing-graphic.htm.

CHAPTER 3: MARTINA NAVRATILOVA

1. Donald McRae, "Interview: Martina Navratilova," *Guardian*,

Nov. 16, 2003, https://www.theguardian.com/sport/2003/nov/17/tennis.donaldmcrae.

2. Ibid.

3. Ibid.

4. Steve Tignor, "1975: Martina Navratilova Defects While Playing in the U.S. Open," Tennis.com, May 7, 2015, http://www.tennis.com/pro-game/2015/05/1975-martina-navratilova-defects-us-while-playing-us-open/54840/.

5. Ibid.

6. Julie Bindel, "Martina Navratilova: I Want to Save Lives," *Guardian*, April 15, 2010, https://www.theguardian.com/sport/2010/apr/15/want-save-lives-martina-navratilova.

7. Ibid.

8. Ibid.

CHAPTER 4: ARNOLD SCHWARZENEGGER

1. Yo Zushi, "Life Lessons from Arnold," *New Statesman*, July 2, 2015, http://www.newstatesman.com/culture/2015/07/life-lessons-arnold-schwarzenegger.

2. Ibid.

3. "Arnold Schwarzenegger Makes Surprise Childhood Revelation," *Hello Magazine*, Sept. 27, 2016, http://us.hellomagazine.com/celebrities/2016092733731/arnold-schwarzenegger-reveals-difficult-childhood/.

4. Arnold Schwarzenegger, "Arnold's Perspectives," schwarzenegger.com, May 23, 2008, http://schwarzenegger.com/.

5. John Preston, "An Austrian Hick in London: Arnie's Early Years," *Telegraph*, July 1, 2015, http://www.telegraph.co.uk/film/terminator-genisys/arnold-schwarzenegger-early-life-bodybuilding/.

6. Ibid.

CHAPTER 5: TAMBA HALI

1. Paul Attner, "By the Grace of God I'm Alive," Sporting News, April 13, 2006, https://web.archive.org/web/20060910022802/http://www.sportingnews.com/yourturn/viewtopic.php?t=82586.
2. Paolo Bandini, "Chiefs Linebacker Tamba Hali: From War-torn Liberia to NFL Glory," *Guardian*, Oct. 10, 2013, https://www.theguardian.com/sport/2013/oct/10/kansas-city-chiefs-linebacker-tamba-hali.
3. Paul Attner, "By the Grace of God I'm Alive."
4. Ibid.
5. Paolo Bandini, "Chiefs Linebacker Tamba Hali: From War-torn Liberia to NFL Glory."
6. Terez Paylor, "Tamba Hali: When I Hit the Field I'm Ready to Go," *Kansas City Star*, Aug. 30, 2016, http://www.kansascity.com/sports/nfl/kansas-city-chiefs/article98885647.html.
7. Paolo Bandini, "Chiefs Linebacker Tamba Hali: From War-torn Liberia to NFL Glory."

CHAPTER 6: MARIA SHARAPOVA

1. David Jones, "The Dark Obsessions that Drove Maria Sharapova's Obsession to Win and Get Rich," *Daily Mail*, March 9, 2016, http://www.dailymail.co.uk/news/article-3483142/DAVID-JONES-dark-past-drove-Maria-Sharapova-s-obsession-win-rich.html.
2. Oliver Brown, "Maria Sharapova Returns to Her Roots in the Wasteland of Chernobyl," *Telegraph*, August 19, 2010, http://www.telegraph.co.uk/sport/tennis/mariasharapova/7952877/Maria-Sharapova-returns-to-her-roots-in-the-wasteland-of-Chernobyl.html.
3. "Sharapova Relives Childhood in Sochi," Tennis.com, February

5, 2014, http://www.tennis.com/pro-game/2014/02/sharapova-relives-childhood-memories-sochi/50516/.

4. David Jones, "The Dark Obsessions that Drove Maria Sharapova's Obsession to Win and Get Rich."

5. Liz Clarke, "Sharapova Wins Wimbledon After Improbable Journey," *Washington Post*, July 4, 2004, http://www.washingtonpost.com/wp-dyn/articles/A25495-2004Jul3.html.

6. Ibid.

7. Inti Kalnins, "Ban on Melodonium May Increase Deaths Among Athletes," Reuters, March 9, 2016, https://www.rt.com/sport/335059-meldonium-inventor-doping-sharapova/.

8. Associated Press, "Maria Sharapova: The Fears and Concerns of My Return," *New York Post*, March 29, 2017, http://nypost.com/2017/03/29/maria-sharapova-the-fears-and-concerns-of-my-return/.

CHAPTER 7: PATRICK EWING

1. Roy S. Johnson, "A Favorite Son Goes Home," *New York Times*, August, 8, 1985, http://www.nytimes.com/1985/08/08/sports/a-favorite-son-goes-home.html.

2. Ibid.

3. "Patrick Ewing Quotes," Brainyquotes.com, https://www.brainyquote.com/quotes/authors/p/patrick_ewing.html.

4. Curtis Bunn, "Journey Recalls Racism for Ewing," *Seattle Times*, Sept. 11, 1994, http://community.seattletimes.nwsource.com/archive/?date=19940911&slug=1929905.

5. Matt Norlander, "Patrick Ewing Says KKK Rally Why He Didn't Attend UNC," CBS Sports, June 13, 2013, http://www.cbssports.com/college-basketball/news/patrick-ewing-says-kkk-rally-partly-why-he-didnt-attend-unc/.

6. Clifton Brown, "The Knicks Private Powerhouse," *New York Times*, April 30, 1993, http://www.nytimes.com/1993/04/30/sports/pro-

basketball-knicks-private-powerhouse-ewing-wants-be-enigma-wrapped-title.html?pagewanted=all.

CHAPTER 8: MARIANO RIVERA

1. Juan Zamorano, "Rivera's Long Ride from a Pacific Fishing Village," *Omaha World Record*, Sept. 20, 2013, http://www.omaha.com/sports/national/rivera-s-long-ride-from-a-pacific-fishing-village/article_ee3f6694-e96a-5924-a0d2-a2eaad4dd472.html.
2. David Waldstein, "The Boyhood Tides that Formed Baseball's Sandman," *New York Times*, Sept. 25, 2013, http://www.nytimes.com/2013/09/26/sports/baseball/the-boyhood-tides-that-formed-baseballs-sandman.html.
3. Juan Zamorano, "Rivera's Long Ride from a Pacific Fishing Village."
4. Michael Bamberger, "Strikeouts by the Boatload," *Sports Illustrated*, March 24, 1997, https://www.si.com/vault/1997/03/24/224695/strikeouts-by-the-boatload-coolheaded-mariano-rivera-is-ready-to-bring-the-heat-as-the-new-closer-for-the-yankees#.
5. Ibid.
6. Ibid.
7. Claire Smith, "Rivera Completes 'No Hitter' in Victory," *New York Times*, April 29, 1996, http://www.nytimes.com/1996/04/29/sports/baseball-rivera-completes-no-hitter-in-victory.html.

GLOSSARY

athleticism Having the traits of fitness, strength, and agility.

banned Disallowed or prohibited.

broadcast To transmit a signal on the radio or television.

catapult To hurl something up and out.

climate The typical weather conditions of an area.

depression Feelings of extreme sadness.

dispersed Distributed over an area.

durability Being able to withstand wear and tear.

fallout Radioactive particles in the air after an explosion.

influential Persuasive.

instability The state of being unpredictable or unreliable.

intellectual Having to do with the brain and thinking.

intimidating Describes having a scary presence in order to get what is wanted.

oppressive Extremely harsh and unjust.

preserving Taking care of something to keep it from changing.

prestigious Respected and important.

psychology The science of mind and behavior.

refuge A safe place.

sophisticated Having experience and knowledge of culture.

stamina The strength to last a long time.

stemming Coming from or originating from.

tenacity The quality of being fierce and unrelenting.

FURTHER READING

BOOKS

Bildner, Phil, and Brett Helquist. *Martina and Chrissie: The Greatest Rivalry in the History of Sports.* London, UK: Candlewick Press, 2017.

Brooke, Phillip. *Dikembe Mutombo: Mount Mutombo.* New York, NY: Children's Press, 1996.

Fischer, David, and Dave Anderson. *Facing Mariano Rivera: Players Recall the Greatest Relief Pitcher Who Ever Lived.* New York, NY: Sports Publishing, 2014.

Geoffreys, Clayton. *Patrick Ewing: The Remarkable Story of One of 90s Basketball Greatest Centers.* Create Space Independent Publishing Platform, 2014.

Lamb, Seth, and Tim Ellsworth. *Pujols Revisited and Updated: More than the Game.* Nashville, TN: Nelson Publishers, 2012.

Mattern, Joanne. *Albert Pujols: Baseball Superstar.* New York, NY: Sports Illustrated Books, 2011.

Mookherji, Kalyani. *Martina Navratilova.* New Delhi, India: Prabhat Prakashan Publishers, 2016.

Pulaski, Mike, and Arnold Schwarzenegger. *Arnold Schwarzenegger Blueprint: The Life Changing Lessons of Arnold Schwarzenegger.* Amazon Digital Services LLC, 2014.

Rivera, Mariano, and Wayne Coffey. *The Closer: Young Reader's Edition.* New York, NY: Little Brown & Co., 2016.

Savage, Jeff. *Maria Sharapova, Amazing Athlete.* Minneapolis, MN: Lerner Publications, 2014.

Seigerman, David. *Tamba Hali.* New York, NY: Aladdin Books, 2017.

Sharapova, Maria. *My Life So Far.* New York, NY: Sarah Crichton Books, 2017.

Torres, John Albert. *Sports Great Dikembe Mutombo.* Berkeley Heights, NJ: Enslow Publishers, 2000.

WEBSITES

Baseball Hall of Fame

baseballhall.org/

The official website of the National Baseball Hall of Fame, a nonprofit organization that records and preserves the history of baseball. It also celebrates the sport's greatest players.

Basketball Hall of Fame

hoophall.com/

Started in 1959, the Naismith Basketball Hall of Fame celebrates the history of basketball and its star athletes. The hall is named after James Naismith, the man credited with inventing basketball.

Tennis Hall of Fame

tennisfame.com/

The International Tennis Hall of Fame preserves and promotes the history of tennis around the world and celebrates its top players.

US Citizenship and Immigration Services

uscis.gov/

The official government website that covers immigration to the United States and ways to become a citizen. The site also provides applications to people interested in becoming permanent US residents.

US Immigration and Customs Enforcement (ICE)

ice.gov/

ICE is the government agency responsible for enforcing immigration. Officials deport immigrants living in the country without legal paperwork to do so.

INDEX

ABOUT THE AUTHOR

JOHN A. TORRES

John A. Torres is an award-winning journalist and writer. He has authored more than sixty books for various publishers. His reporting has taken him all over the world. He has filed stories from Indonesia, India, Zambia, Italy, Mexico, and Haiti, among others.

When John is not writing, he enjoys reading, fishing, spending time with his family, and playing music with his band, the Hemingways.